WHEN DEPRESSION HITS

WHEN

DEPRESSION

HITS

Ricky Roberts III

IP INDEPENDENTLY PUBLISHED

Editor: Jeanie Lyubelsky
Bio Photo: Joey Clay ©
Cover Photo: Imleedh Ali

Published in the United States of America
1. Mental Health / Depression
2. Psychology & Counseling / Mental Illness
23.07.07

CONTENTS

FRIENDLY WARNING

The topic of suicide and other negative thoughts related to depression are shared in this book. The content is intended to encourage you, not to bring you down. However, because I don't know what your mental state may be at this time and the potential sensitivities with talking about depression and suicide, I want to give you a friendly heads-up before you read the pages that follow.

DEDICATION

I dedicate this book to everyone who deals with depression.

PREFACE

This book reflects my experience with depression and the ways I manage it. I wrote it to help myself get through one of the darkest episodes of depression I have had in a long time. It was a way to remind myself of what I do when depression hits and encourage me to keep pushing onward. My greatest hope for this book is that it helps you get through your bouts with depression, like it helped me get through one of mine.

My suggestions within this book are

minimal as compared to how many different practices and actions are available. Ultimately, you will want to find the healthy things that work best for you. In addition to what you can do to help work through waves of depression, you may also have habits and choices that trigger or add to your experience. Addressing those things is equally as important as adopting practices to help you navigate depression when it comes.

Regardless of where you are mentally or what you feel about yourself, take a moment to acknowledge how much you have overcame and worked through up to this point in your life. It matters and deserves recognition. I admire your courage and strength to be here.

INTRODUCTION

Depression ruins and ends people's lives, and it is more than temporarily being in a bad mood. When depression hits, it overpowers you. You experience a sense of numbness and darkness that is hard to manage. It takes a lot of work to push through depression onsets.

Sometimes, no matter how hard you try and what you do, the heaviness you feel won't go away. It is like a storm that doesn't seem to stop, because when you think the sun might be coming out, it starts raining again.

I remember first dealing with mild episodes of feeling depressed in elementary school. From middle school on, I began experiencing numbing levels of depression. I had no idea what it was or how to deal with it.

I never wanted to tell people about how bad I felt, the amount of self-harm I did, and the frightening thoughts I often had about taking my life. I felt withdrawn, but I worked hard to pretend that everything was okay. I perfected fake smiles and pretended to be happy. In fact, I still do this more often than I would like to admit.

Understanding my own experience with depression and how to best work through it has been a long journey for me. My efforts to manage my mental health and ongoing dance with depression comprise a lifelong process. Depression is not something that I think I need to remove from my life. Instead, I respect it as something that I coexist with as fluidly and positively as possible.

Despite my personal history with

depression, I cannot claim to understand the severity of your struggles or challenges. This book is not about defining any one aspect of depression or creating the idea that it is all the same. It's about encouraging you to get through your battles with depression in the different ways that they may present themselves to you.

KNOW YOUR WHYS

As dark as your thoughts can get at times, or as strongly you may feel about giving up, knowing your 'whys' will help you keep going. They are the things that motivate and inspire you. Your whys make the troubles and struggles of life feel worth it.

Not only is it important that you know your whys, but also that you think about them often. Being in touch with your whys helps you keep going when you feel like you have lost all will to do so.

There were times in a recent battle with depression when I needed to think about my son, wife, family, friends, and things I care about for the energy I needed to not give up. I was in a dark place. There was a cloud of depression over me that wasn't going to simply drift away. Thinking about my whys was the only thing that kept me going.

The feelings of wanting to give up the fight came in waves, some more intense than others. This particular bout with depression lasted over a year. That season was alarming, because I hadn't been that close to attempting to take my life in many years.

One memorable night, I was having a hard time and felt disconnected from everyone. I could see my wife and son, we were in the same room, but I felt myself slipping away. I told my wife that I was going out for a drive. When I said bye to her and my son, I felt like I was saying it for good.

As I drove around, I couldn't shake the many reasons I told myself that I should end my life. The pace of the distorted thoughts increased.

I was allowing them to take me deeper and deeper into the darkness of depression. While in those moments, my mind had me believing that committing suicide was the right thing to do, even an attractive option.

Eventually, I ended up in a parking lot. I felt like I was in a dream, watching everything happen, numbed and separated from reality. I thought to myself, "This is the time. It is the right thing to do." I consciously let go of any control I tried to maintain over where my mind was taking me. I knew that if I let my thoughts take over, I would end my life.

My body was shaking. I was scared. If there were ten steps to do what was necessary to take my life that night, I was on step number eight.

My mind was sending reasons to do it at a rapid speed. It was happening and felt like swimming upstream against the current after being already exhausted.

I knew I had to shift my thoughts, but I couldn't seem to do so. Then, I managed to call on a tiny glimpse of my son's face. It quickly faded, but it brought me out of the fog enough to know that I had to reach for more visions of my son. I searched for one thought of him at a time.

I slowly began to gain control over my mind, bit by bit. Eventually, I had enough power to think about how taking my life would affect him. I reflected on the idea of him at some point, even considering feeling like he wasn't worth it for me to keep fighting. Yet I thought in the same moment about how I never want such a situation for my son, and I can't do that to him. He is more than worth me pushing through my battle with depression, over and over again.

I also began to think about my wife and how it would make her feel. I then focused on thoughts about my family, our dogs, friends, and other whys I have. Thought by thought, I pulled myself together. After stabilizing myself, I drove home to hug my wife and son. I cried the whole way there and was so happy to see them.

Your reasons to keep going are a lifeline that you can always call on. Even when you have trouble thinking of them, fight to do so with everything you have. I encourage you to reflect on anything that brings you joy, happiness, inspiration, or a sense of belonging.

If you can't identify anything, get things in your life that are important to you. They don't have to be people. They can be anything positive. A pet, plant, hobby, acts of service, a volunteer opportunity you can feel invested in, or anything else that gives you a sense of purpose. It is essential to have things you can lean on or think of when you feel like giving up.

Don't only engage in thinking about your whys when depression hits you. Be involved and think about them often. Bring your awareness to why those people or things matter to you and how they wouldn't be the same without you. The more you do or think about them, the greater will be the barrier that you create against the dark thoughts you need to get past.

As I described in the experience of feeling vulnerable to taking my life, sometimes the dark thoughts flood so rapidly that a barrier can't stop them. When that happens, reach for thoughts of your whys as if your life depends on it. In fact, the more present your reasons to exist are, the less likely dark thoughts will be to pick up enough momentum to take over. In addition, consistent engagement with and reflections on things and people you care about will combat unhealthy ideas as they come.

Believe and know that as important as your identified whys are to you, you are just as important to them. They need you, as does the world. Only one person can bring to the world what you can, the way you can. That person is you.

I honor you for pushing through waves of depression as often as you already have. Don't stop now. Thank you for being here.

KEEP IT MOVING

There are days when I wake up in the morning, and all of the sudden out of nowhere, I feel the weight of depression trying to hold me down. I felt okay when I went to sleep the night before, but by morning it seems like an unmovable weighted blanket is lying on top of me. In other words, I feel numb and have no desire to get out of bed.

I can hear my son playing in his room with my wife through the baby monitor. In my mind, I want to jump out of bed and go see them, but depression is hitting me, and I stay stuck under the covers. At this point, anxiety mounts. I know I need to make a move, because the longer I lay there, the harder it will be to get out of bed. I dig for the will to put my feet on the ground. From there, I can walk to see my wife and son. After that, I go to something else that will give me a sense of empowerment.

I don't think about my whole day when depression is setting in. Instead, I think about one step and keep it moving from there. Little by little, I start piecing my morning together, trying to lift the shadow of depression lingering over me. Eventually, I find myself going through my day, and the feeling of being depressed either subsides or goes away completely.

When I am experiencing an onset of depression, the best I can do is to ease it. Whether I lessen the severity or make it go away for the remainder of the day, keeping it moving is imperative. Furthermore, I don't only keep it moving when I am depressed. I have found that being active, in general, and maintaining uplifting practices help prevent onsets of depression from occurring.

It's important to sit with how you feel. Keeping it moving is not about avoiding dealing with your emotions; rather, it's a matter of not allowing depression to hold you down.

Processing your feelings can be a part of keeping things moving. You are addressing your emotions by focusing on how you feel and reflecting on the decisions you can make to improve your well-being. If you can do nothing about something that is bringing you down, honor the heaviness you feel and find the strength to move forward.

Instead of lying in bed dwelling with no motivation because of depression, find ways to help yourself process the emotions without being stuck in them. I do several things that involve action while processing something I may be going through that is triggering my depression. I utilize writing, drawing, surfing when I can, and meditation, to name a few, in order to facilitate a good mental space for processing things. I also rely heavily on skateboarding to manage my mental health.

Even though I'm putting energy into why I may be feeling depressed while doing things such as journaling, drawing, meditation, and skateboarding, I am still keeping things moving through the actions that I take to do them. The things I do to process my emotions and not be held down by depression all require multiple steps. For example, when I choose to write during a bout with depression, I don't always feel like it. I start writing by acting on one thing at a time.

My steps start with getting my pen and notebook. Such a process may even involve taking care of various responsibilities before I can even take the time to write at all. Whatever the situation, I get started by taking one small step at a time.

The same goes for skateboarding. There are days when I don't feel like skating. I don't feel like seeing or talking to anyone. It's nothing personal against the people I skate with or may see when I am skating. I just generally don't feel like seeing anyone when I am feeling depressed.

The only thing I want to do is to stay in bed or be alone. However, I know that I will feel much better if I skate. So, I move from one small step to the next until I leave my house to go skating.

When you don't have the motivation to do anything because depression is holding you down, then take one action that will help get you going and keep it moving from there. It can be as simple as bringing your knees to your chest and taking one deep breath. Anything to make yourself move. The game is to find one thing to focus your mind on and take action toward it. Then, do something else, then another step, and another.

Eventually, by keeping it moving, you are either taking yourself out of the depths of your depressed state or shaking it off entirely for the time being. Sometimes you are pushing through severe onsets of depression for days or months. Other times it just shows up for a brief period and moves on.

Regardless of the intensity of any depression episode you face, do your best to keep things moving. Don't think about everything you must do for the day, tomorrow, or next week. Instead, focus on moving yourself out from underneath the blanket of depression that is lying over you. Then, once you get it lifted, keep pushing on by doing one thing at a time.

ADDRESS IT PROACTIVELY

Episodes of depression do not go away on their own. If you do nothing about them, they will not stop and often will get worse. If you had a sprained ankle, you would take care of it. If you were suffering from a toothache, you would do something about it. If you cut open your finger, you would bandage it or get stitches if necessary. The list of things that you would not ignore if they happened could go on and on.

Unfortunately, people don't always give

mental health the attention it needs. Instead, they allow themselves to get stuck in a state of being depressed. Some people are even comfortable with the way depression feels. Whatever the case, when you battle depression, you can lose touch with what it is like to be genuinely happy.

Your mental health deserves the same sense of priority and urgency as every other aspect of your existence. When your mental well-being is not good, it harms every part of your life.

Do not leave depression be as if it will go away or ease up on its own. It is not a common cold that runs its course and then you feel better. Depression needs your attention when it is showing its face and when everything is fine.

Doing things to address depression when it hits you helps ease the severity and eventually sends it away for a while. When you are proactive about the possibility of depression returning at any time, the time between episodes gets longer. Although you may not be able to avoid ever being depressed again, you can do things today that will keep it away or send it off if you are experiencing it in real time.

How you deal with depression is up to you. As long as you do something healthy that does not hurt yourself or others, there is no right or wrong way to handle it. Manage your dance with depression in ways that work for you and are easily accessible and sustainable.

I tend to depression, whether active or not, in the same way. When I am depressed, I consider what I do as tools to get me out of the fog. But, on the other hand, when my mental health is good, I think of the things I do as prevention.

As I mentioned, how you manage your depression is up to you. If you don't have activities, hobbies, and practices that help you work through waves of depression, I encourage you to find some. Your method may be anything that requires movement, gives you a sense of purpose and belonging, takes focus, and facilitates well-being.

It's not about what you do to take care of your mental health and address depression. It's about having the tools and practices in place and keeping them as an active part of your life. If you already have things you do to maintain your mental health, keep doing them.

Depression is a powerful thing. It can make you feel in ways that are unexplainable and have you thinking thoughts about hurting yourself that can be terrifying. Don't ignore or dismiss it.

When a wave of depression starts to show up, address it with every self-care and positive mental health tool you have. Even if you're doing the things known to help you shake it off and you still feel bad, keep doing them. Although it's easy to think that the things you're doing are not working, imagine how bad it would be if you weren't doing them.

The less proactive you are about addressing depression, the more precious moments of life depression will keep you from enjoying. You are worthy of happiness. Never forget that.

BE KIND TO YOURSELF

B eing mean and hurtful to yourself does you no good. However, when you are kind to yourself, you will start to feel better organically. Being kind to yourself is not always easy, but it is necessary for your well-being.

You may have regrets or guilt from choices you made in the past or are not happy with during your life. None of us are perfect, and sometimes our lives are not what we want them to be. Whatever the case, being unkind to yourself will do nothing to change what happened and will only make you more depressed than you already may be.

Imagine a clear glass of water. The clarity of the water symbolizes a positive, happy state of being. However, the water darkens if you add a small amount of black food coloring. The food coloring represents depression, and the small amount added to the water represents depression slowly showing its face.

Every time you say or think a negative thought about yourself, more drops of black food coloring get added to the water. As time goes on and the more hurtful you are to yourself, the darker the water gets until it is solid black. In other words, your thoughts and self-talk make the onset of depression worse, not better.

On the other hand, when you speak positively to yourself and about yourself while practicing self-care, you add more water instead of black food coloring. Being kind to yourself will help to dilute the food coloring. In other words, it will help dissolve the current wave of depression.

A wide range of things and behaviors can

make a depressed state worse. Not being kind to yourself is only one of them. In the same way that there are many things you can do to yourself to make an episode with depression worse, there are also activities other than being kind to yourself that will help you work through a battle with depression.

Ultimately, anything you do to help with your depression starts with how you treat yourself. Being kind to yourself enables you to feel more motivated to do more activities, such as exercising, writing, drawing, doing yoga, dancing, meditating, and eating healthily—to name some—that will help you feel better.

Be diligent about treating yourself kindly. This may be difficult and uncomfortable initially, but it is worth the effort. Not only will you feel better within, but those around you will also benefit.

You are worthy of everything great that this world has to offer. You deserve to be healthy and happy. I encourage you to treat yourself in ways that align with those truths.

ONE THING AT A TIME

When depression is hitting, try to focus on the small steps you can take, one at a time, to help get you through it. It's a lot like what I mentioned earlier about choosing one simple thing to get moving and build from there. Don't get overwhelmed by figuring out how to not be depressed.

When you are deep in depression, it can feel like there is no way out. You can feel hopeless. In that state of being, it is hard to conceive what you can do to help yourself feel better.

Even when you have ideas, it's hard to know where to begin. On the other hand, even if you have insight on where to start, it is not uncommon to feel a lack of motivation to do anything about it anyway. You can think of what to do but struggle to begin, making you feel bad about yourself—and intensify the depression.

You desire to shake a cloud of depression when it has come over you. You want to feel good again. It's a matter of doing the things that will help you get there.

Start adding one thing to your life daily that will lift your mood. It doesn't have to be anything grand or take a long time. Even if it is only doing something for five minutes, it will help. The key is to do it. Not only will whatever it is that you choose to do every day help you feel good, but it will also build your confidence by sticking to doing something you told yourself you would do.

After successfully incorporating one positive thing into your daily practice, think of one more activity or healthy habit to add to your day or week that will elevate your mood. You can slowly add more from there once you consistently do what you have already added.

Whether you add physical activities, therapeutic art practices, healthier eating habits, or whatever else you see fit, you are combating depression by incorporating positive actions into your daily life that will help you feel better. As you include more uplifting habits, you will begin to feel up more than you do down. As a result, over time, the depressed state will slowly start to dissipate or at least ease up significantly.

Staying depressed becomes more difficult when you prioritize doing things that help make you smile while feeling healthy and good about yourself. Everything you add to help you push through depression is on your terms. If you only have five minutes per day for each added activity or can only do something once per week, it's okay. The activities and habits you choose must work well for your schedule, or you won't keep doing them.

Do one positive thing and keep adding more as you can. Don't add so many that you get stressed about keeping up. The goal is to feel better, not overwhelmed. So even if you only add one positive thing to your life that makes you feel better, it will help.

You may be surprised by how adding one thing will naturally inspire you to add another. For example, when you feel happy because of something you started doing, you will want to spend more time in that activity or even add more things to your life that will make you feel good.

Depression can be challenging to manage. It makes you feel anxious, afraid, and sometimes hopeless. Get past it one step at a time when you are in that space. Do one thing that will help you gain control over how you feel and move forward from there.

THE DANCE

The demands of life do not stop when you are in the midst of depression. The need to take care of your many responsibilities and maintain your relationships is always there. So as much as you may feel like lying in bed all day, you can't.

When you have zero motivation and feel numb to the world, it takes a lot of effort to function and interact with others. Even if you have people near you with whom you can be open with about your depression, you do not want to bring them down, so you try not to talk about it. As far as the rest of the world is concerned, you almost always try to hide how you're feeling, as best as you can. Either way, there is a constant dance between dealing with what you feel on the inside and intentionally concealing it, so others don't know you are depressed or get impacted negatively.

None of this is to say that there are no moments when your depression affects the mood of others because of the way it is affecting yours. When you are depressed, sometimes it's hard to be anything else but that. Often it manifests in just being quiet and mopey. But, on the other hand, it can lead to outbursts, being negative, or having an attitude and shortness with others. When this happens, be easy on yourself.

I have let my depression bring down my wife's vibe, and I am sure many others, many times. Although I do my best not to let the waves of depression that come over me be a burden to others, it still happens. So the dance becomes to honor how you feel while also being mindful not to project it out too much.

I am not saying that you should avoid being vulnerable or honest with your feelings. Those things are crucial and should be a part of your life. It is about doing them while also acknowledging your depression. Yet, at the same time, we want to stay aware of not bringing others down or treating them poorly because of being depressed.

As I mentioned, there may be times when you are so deep in your depression that you can't help but bring others down and even lash out. It doesn't make it right, but unfortunately, it does happen. The goal is to find harmony with acknowledging your feelings while not allowing your depression to bring down those around you. It is not an easy dance, but it is undoubtedly worth practicing.

PAY ATTENTION TO YOUR THOUGHTS

Depression tends to hit us off guard. One moment you are happy, and the next, you feel like you are struggling to breathe. When that happens, there is little you can do beyond using the healthy tools and practices that help you push through the heaviness of depression. But, on the other hand, depression can creep in slowly, gradually chipping away at your well-being until it takes you down.

Whether depression blindsides you or approaches slowly, it is essential to pay attention to your thoughts regularly. The sooner you acknowledge and adjust negative thinking, the easier it is to keep yourself away from a gradual onset of depression, and you will find yourself in a better position to manage an episode when it hits you by surprise. Negative thoughts can lead you into a funk and keep you there when depression hits without warning. On the other hand, positive thinking can help keep you from getting depressed and take you out of a depression episode when you suddenly find yourself in one.

When you pay attention to your thoughts, you can change them as they become negative or otherwise unhealthy. Adjusting your mental attitude from negative to positive isn't always easy and can take a lot of effort. It's not about being perfect, either. It's an ongoing work in progress. Be patient with yourself and do your best.

Your thoughts are like pieces of a puzzle coming together one at a time to shape the state of your mental health. You can be a proactive participant in this process. You can change where your thoughts are taking you at any time. However, when you aren't paying attention to them, they can take control of your mindset.

There are times when I follow my negative thoughts into dark places. When this happens, the next thing I know, I am feeling depressed. Sometimes my way of thinking gets out of control, and I am taking small steps to prepare for a suicide attempt. When this happens, I am not paying attention to the many thoughts that lead me to such a scary state. My mind takes control when I am not harnessing my strength and ability to direct my thoughts.

A few weeks before writing this section, I felt myself slipping all day. I was not actively involved in what my mind was doing or where it was taking me, and I was spiraling emotionally and mentally.

Later that night, I sat alone in my garage. I knew I was a bit down, but I didn't realize how deep I had slipped into depression throughout the day. The longer I sat there, the more how I felt caught up to me. My thoughts were racing from one worry about negative things to the next.

Then, suddenly, I stared at an extension cord on the floor. Then I looked up at the exposed beam across the garage ceiling and focused on a cooler I could stand on. My mind quickly put the three together and flashed the sequential actions of wrapping the extension cord around the beam, googling how to tie a noose knot, tying one around my neck, standing on the cooler, and taking a final step. Every step I imagined seemed so easy.

From there, I looked at the notebook on my desk in the garage, opened it, and began writing a farewell letter. Assessing what I would use, thinking of a plan, and starting the note all happened within minutes. My thoughts in those moments were taking me to the edge of taking my life. As I walked toward the extension cord, I reached desperately for anything that would help me shift my mind.

Fortunately, I changed my thoughts in what I felt was just in time. I held onto flickering visions of my son laughing. I ran past the extension cord and out of the garage into my house.

When I got inside, I sat in my office in a daze with my heart racing as if I had just escaped being attacked by someone. Once I settled down, I pushed myself to become present with where my mind was at. I reflected on how little I had been in tune with my thoughts and feelings throughout the day. Even though I know how important it is to be more diligent about paying attention to any signs, ideas, and behaviors that are likely to take me to a dark and dangerous place, I still slip up.

Sometimes you know when you are walking toward the dark cloud of depression instead of away from it. Other times, as I noted earlier, there are days when one minute you're happy, and the next you're struggling to keep going. Whatever the case, awareness of your thoughts, responses to people and situations, and how you feel inside is vital.

Pay attention to how many negative thoughts you are focusing on. Be aware of if you're experiencing irritability. Take note when you start lashing out at those you love. Are you getting annoyed easier than usual? Do you feel anxious? Are you experiencing shortness of breath? Do you feel tired and unmotivated? Any one of these things, and other symptoms of depression, are imperative to address as quickly as possible.

At times it feels impossible to do anything about the symptoms of depression or the things that take you toward being depressed. You might feel powerless to do anything at all. But I assure you, even when you don't feel like you can fight the thoughts, change your mood, or alter your physical turmoil, you can. You have the power!

Reach for any positive thoughts or a reflection of a good memory you have with someone. From there, grasp for another one and keep going. The idea is to pay attention to how you think and feel while making adjustments when necessary. The more involved you are with your thoughts, the easier it is to manage your existence with depression.

YOU ARE NOT ALONE

One of the hardest things for me to deal with when I am depressed is how much of a burden I feel like I am. I don't usually tell anyone what I am working through because of this thought. I generally try to minimize my interactions with people when I am depressed. I don't want what I am feeling to bring them down.

No matter how much I try to disguise being depressed, it can still show, and others can feel it. Furthermore, as much as I want to hide it, sometimes I don't have the energy to do so. During those times, I work extra hard to keep some distance between myself and the people otherwise close to me.

As I have mentioned, I do different things to combat my depression. Most of them, I do away from people, and some, I do around others. One of the many things I do to help with my depression is to go skateboarding.

Something I love about skateboarding is that when I am deep into an onset of depression, I can get lost in a battle to land a trick or skate in general and feel my depression fall away. The beauty is that I can skate with others and still connect with them but have minimal conversations. It's as if I can be alone to some degree but still feel support from others.

Some people may not understand what it's like for you to deal with depression. Others may question why you can't just snap out of it. They might even say things like, "You are not doing enough. Everyone has bad days. Get over it." When you feel people don't get it or they say things that are dismissive of what you're dealing with, you may feel more shame than you already do. If you could snap out of it, do more, or get over it, you would.

It takes much more effort to shake clouds of depression than most people realize. Whether people understand what it's like to fight depression as you do, or whatever minimizing comment they make when you are down, it doesn't matter. You know what it's like and how hard you work to push through those darker days when they come. And you don't need their approval or understanding.

Yet it hurts to hear others say dismissive things when you are struggling. Unfortunately, you can't change how people that don't experience depression see it or how they'll respond. However, those who work so hard to manage it, and those who continue to master it, appreciate the battle.

Ultimately, it is not about how others treat you or don't. It is about you believing in your importance in this world. Your existence matters and is a contribution to humanity.

It is okay to be depressed. Push through it

the best that you can. Don't let anyone's lack of care or hurtful comments blind you from seeing the outstanding person that you are. No matter how much you feel like a burden to others at times, you are not; those very people you care about, also care about you.

Be proud of yourself for making it this far. Honor how many times you have gotten back up from being depressed. Celebrate everything you have learned and accomplished up to this point in your life.

You are a gift to this world.

GIVE YOURSELF GRACE

Dealing with depression makes you feel powerless at times. You want to feel better but can't seem to shake it. When that is the case, it often causes frustration. The frustration then turns into anger toward yourself.

Regardless of how others may think about you for being depressed, it will never be as bad as you judge yourself. On that note, it is easy to spiral deeper into depression when your self-talk becomes hurtful and discouraging.

Before long, you are convincing yourself that you are worthless.

My mind becomes such a harsh environment when depression hits. I get so angry at myself, especially at times when I feel like I should be happy. I tend to think poorly about myself in those moments. I despise who I am when my mood brings down those around me. That is the last thing I ever want to do or mean to do.

I encourage you to give yourself grace as you work through your struggles. Dealing with depression is tiring and overwhelming enough on its own as a nonstop battle. So it's okay to be tired and discouraged.

Managing depression is complex, and it takes hard work to process everything that comes with it. Keep in mind to give yourself grace for falling and not always being at your best when you are feeling unmotivated and don't want to see or talk with anyone.

You are an incredible human being. The fact that you have pushed through so many onsets of depression, often in silence and alone, is worthy of much praise. Your strength and courage are admirable.

Never stop pushing, and always give yourself grace along the way. I believe in you.

CLOSING STATEMENT

Even on the hardest days, if you dig deep enough, you will find the strength and courage to continue the fight. Your existence is worth you doing everything it takes to never give up.

Keep up the good push, always.

REFLECTIONS

_____

_____

_____

_____

_____

_____

_____

_____

_____

_____

_____

_____

_____

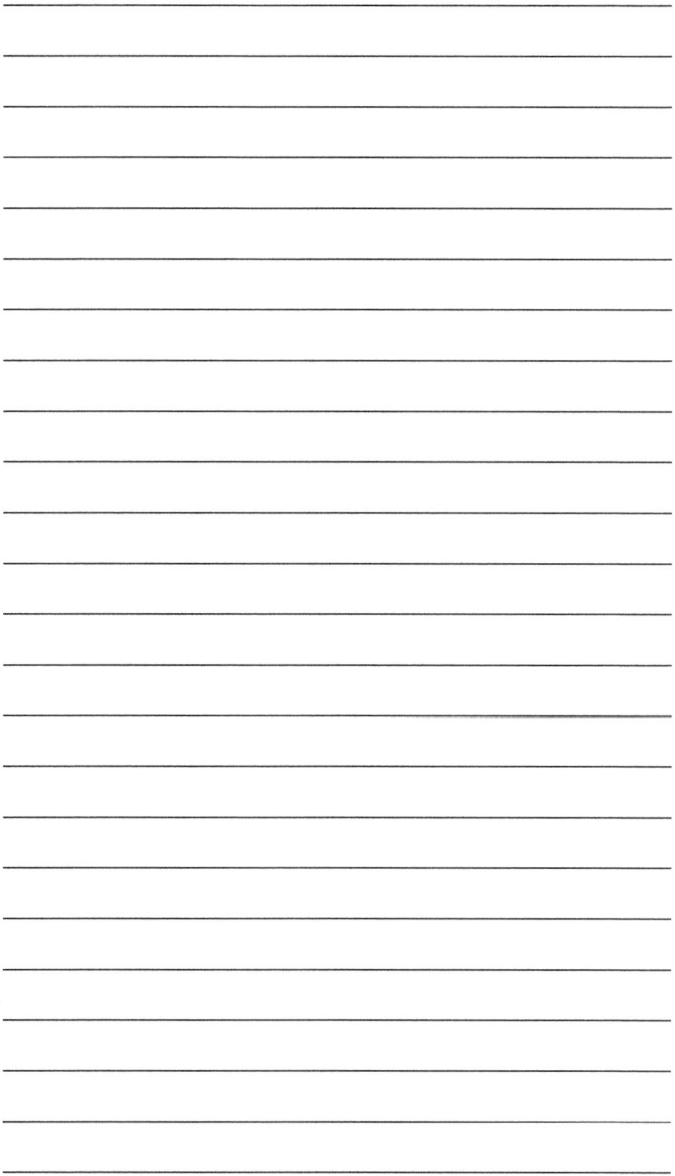

OTHER BOOKS BY RICKY ROBERTS III

- *You* (2004)

- *What Really Matters?* (2006)

- *Where Did the Gift Go?* (2009)

- *Awakening the New You: A Path to Transformation* (2013)

- *Just for Youth (2015)*

- *Healing the Wounded Child Within: Heal Your Wounds Change Your Life* (2018)

- *Far Fom Easy: What It Takes to Make Your Dreams a Reality* (2019)

- *Thank You Skateboarding* (2020)